Youniverse

Copyright © 2019 Tajinder Kaur Sekhon/Ritu Kaur is the copyright claimant and author.

Cover design by Jasmeet Singh. © 2019 Tajinder Kaur Sekhon.

All rights reserved. No part of this publication may be reproduced, stored in a retrieval system, or transmitted in any form or by any means, electronic, mechanical, photocopying, recording, or otherwise, without written permission of the publisher and author.

ISBN-13: 978-0-578-56599-6
ISBN-10: 0-578-56599-4

And now I'm 25. We think for some reason with each year that passes by, we're going to be older. Or feel older. Yes we do get older but many of us still feel the same. I am all ages at different parts of my life. When I'm weeping in my mother's arms I'm eight. When I'm eating roti with mirch dha achaar at 3am, I'm three years old waiting for my father to come home from work so we can eat together. When I'm looking at the world without judgment I'm twelve. I can regress back to a certain age when needed, but don't we all? Even though I'm 25 now, don't I act a certain age at specific parts of my life for familiarity, for comfort? I do. I think we all do. Like the times he used to drink coke nonstop when he first came to America because he didn't have the privilege of drinking it when he was in the motherland. And how years of drinking soda took the enamel off his teeth. We forget about moderation. But the coke gets replaced with alcohol when we get older. Weeping in my mother's arms turns to crying myself to sleep so that she doesn't have to feel my pain. And this is when I know I'm 25.

— *The Excerpt I Wrote For "Youniverse" When I Was 25*

Youniverse

Ritu Kaur

Youniverse

The waves brought me here

Ritu Kaur

Youniverse
Is *your universe*
You hold the ability
To create your reality

Youniverse

As humans we hurt each other tremendously. And in the process, we're also hurting Mother Nature and Earth simultaneously. I love our planet. I love nature. And I am so thankful for being here. For being granted this captivating life. So I'd like to take this moment to apologize. I am sorry. I am sorry for every single time I have taken you for granted, Mother Earth. I am sorry for not waking up to see you rise every morning. I am sorry for seeming unappreciative while living in your home, Earth. 'Cause you are my temporary home in this life. So instead of just apologizing for not treating you better, I want to take this moment to thank you, dear mother. 'Cause deep down I am grateful. I am thankful. I am stunned by Earth's beauty again and again. From every sunrise to each sunset. With each flower that blooms in conditions where it seems like nothing is able to thrive. Mother Nature, you astound me over and over with your radiating beauty and strength. You are my mother and my home. And I am blessed to be able to share this divine feminine energy with you. The energy and blessing of creation.

— *We Must Do Better For Mother Earth*

Ritu Kaur

Yelling is not necessary
Nor allowed
Here

Youniverse

The salt water
The salt water
The salt water in the ocean
The salt water
The salt water
The salt water in my eyes
Is proof that we're all different forms
Of the sea

Ritu Kaur

Never liked wine until I met you

Youniverse

He told me my eyes seek attention
I told him
No one's but his

Ritu Kaur

There's something magnetic about you

— *Proton & Electron*

Youniverse

I was 24, you were 25
We were friends, best friends
I told you to be ready in 20 minutes
It was New Year's Eve
I was sitting on the roof of my car before I went back down to sit on your lap while you were in the passenger seat
I miss those times, I miss those times
We'd been drinking fireball in the car and talking even though we should've been inside the house party
We'd lost track of time
The clock was about to strike midnight
We got out of the car quickly
And it was no longer 2016
I was rushing inside the house party while you were running behind me
You said *New Year's kiss* and then melted into me
Our New Year's kiss was in the middle of the street
Neither of us had ever had a New Year's kiss before
I think that's what made it feel more special
We were drunk when we went inside
We danced while more booze went down our throats
About an hour later we were ready to go
I could barely walk so you walked behind me for support
You felt warm
Like love
We got inside the car and it was the first time for me
The way it happened naturally
It felt like it happened magically
Parts of that night are still a blur to me
But I wouldn't change a single thing about what happened between you and me

— *The First Time*

Ritu Kaur

It's hard to imagine life without you
You agreed with me
Stated you knew the feeling all too well
And left me there anyway

Youniverse

We all hurt each other
Whether by intention or not
What's important to keep in mind is that intention
'Cause you were aware of what you were doing
And you still continued doing it for months
So tell me how the universe
Is supposed to forget something like that
Tell me
Tell me
Tell me
Life is a circle
Did you forget
Whatever we give out, we receive
And it's sad how most people forget this
Including you

Ritu Kaur

You were guilty of doing the things
You falsely accused me of
Yet I'm the one who ended up with
Trust issues

— *Projection*

Youniverse

I was willing to leave my world
Just to be a part of yours

— *How Naive Of Me*

Ritu Kaur

I am not a backup plan
I am not insurance for your ego
If you can't choose what you want
There is a door to decide for you

— *Not Your Second Option*

Youniverse

Beating yourself up
For loving someone deeply
Is not your fault
It's their loss for not being ready for
A love as pure as yours

Ritu Kaur

The thing about almost-lovers
Is the uncertainty
It's the mystery that leaves you wondering
What if
It's the heartbreak no one warns you about
When you're wide awake at 4am
Missing someone who was never yours

Youniverse

And what am I to do with these
Leftover feelings for you
That creep up on me unexpectedly
Just when I thought I was over you

Ritu Kaur

We were so close
Or were we

— *Delusions*

Youniverse

I still talk to you every now and then
During my walks
Or when I'm venting to you on my drive home
Or when I'm singing songs to you
While I'm in the shower
Or trying to get these words on paper that are too shy
To come out
It's been months since I last heard your voice
But my conversations with you
Haven't stopped

— Coping Mechanism For When I Miss You

When you're consumed with overthinking
With over analyzing
With obsessing over what went wrong
I hope you find solace in the fact that
There is nothing
You could have done differently
If they wanted to be with you
They would be

— It's That Simple

Youniverse

He's taken care of himself
It's your turn to do the same

Ritu Kaur

Love is about
Compromises
Not one sided
Sacrifices

Youniverse

I've found people are most honest
During departures
A kiss goodbye at the airport
A last fight
A final farewell
Death

Ritu Kaur

I miss you on the good days too
'Cause you're still the first one I want to tell
My good news to

Youniverse

We're laughing like we always did
But there's small talk this time, brief silences
Until I tell you I've got to get going
You weren't ready for me to say that
You pause then finally utter
It's November and you know what that means
Another brief pause
I'm engaged now, Ritu
I wanted to share that with you
I smile and congratulate you
How do you feel
You smile weakly at my question
Big change, I feel a big change
You don't give many details
I congratulate you once more
Are you happy
This question creeps into my mind but I don't ask
I still get my answer when you show up unannounced
To my favorite teahouse while hiding your left hand
I get my answer when I see the ring on your finger
one minute
And when it's no longer there the next
'Cause you took it off secretly
Thinking I wouldn't notice
Do you think about me?
You catch me off guard with this question
Think about what? I ask
Me
You utter so quickly, I can hear the anticipation
In your voice
No, I don't think about irrelevant things
I look down, trying to think up a joke
You smile that sad smile
I still think about you
I've missed you
I miss you
You tell me things that no longer matter

Ritu Kaur

I look back down again
Look up back at you
Well, I am a 'missable' person
Is the best reply I can think of at the moment
You agree and start complimenting me
How do I tell you that I still love you
But I've let you go for my own peace
'Cause you're the one who decided I wasn't for you
Yet you're the one who showed up to my
Favorite tea house uninvited
Telling me things that no longer make sense
Do you finally feel what I was feeling
Do you finally understand what I was trying so long
To tell you
Are you happy
No longer lingers in my mind
It's none of my business
Not anymore

Youniverse

At one point I said you were my youniverse

Ritu Kaur

I wanted to spend my life writing poetry for you
You were my poetry in human form

— *For Someone Else*

Youniverse

Counting down the days
We had together
Was like watching the sand
Trickle down to the other side
Of the hourglass

— *A Different Type Of Death*

Ritu Kaur

Someday I'll be thousands of miles away from home
Snorkeling on a beach somewhere in Southeast Asia
And you'll be living your life as well
Doing whatever makes you happy
And it'll be crazy that we live in the same world
While being thousands of miles apart
That even though we may not talk anymore
We'll have had history together
History that we can revisit in our minds
History which will remain just that
History
'Cause we will no longer have the choice
Of taking that history and
Recreating it for a future moment

Youniverse

Sometimes you unknowingly visit
A place for the last time
Whether it's a place
A person
Or a feeling

Ritu Kaur

It isn't always necessary
To see them one last time
For closure

— *Closure Comes From Within*

Youniverse

Don't ask the higher power for signs
If you're going to ignore them
When they come

Ritu Kaur

Right now I deeply wish we worked out, but I know there's a greater reason for why we didn't. And by then we'll only be fragments of each other who surface up in one another's memories once in a while, wondering what if. But I think and hope we'll be in better places than that a few years later; where a brief smell may give me a vivid flashback of you with a good aftertaste, which makes me smile and think of you as a great friend from a different time.

— 2/3 Of The Three Loves Theory

Youniverse

He may have lied to you about many things
But when he tells you
He doesn't want to be in a relationship
Believe him
He may sweet talk you into thinking
You're the only one but
When he says he's not ready for a relationship
He's not ready for a relationship with you
If there's one thing he's telling you the truth about
It's his indirect disinterest towards you
He may have known how to get you
But he never planned to keep you
So when he gives you any reason
For why you can't be
You must leave

Ritu Kaur

By the time the woman of your dreams comes along
You've had a heartbreak or two
And you don't know what to do with her
So you end up losing her

— *The One Who Got Away*

Youniverse

No man's excuses are worth my time
When I've witnessed my stepfather
Wait
Ten years
For my mother

Ritu Kaur

You said you wanted to give me the world
But I wanted to give you the youniverse

— *The Difference*

Youniverse

And when we embraced in a hug
You took in my scent one last time
A long, deep breath in
And right away I knew
I'd never see you again

Ritu Kaur

Dear Ritu,

I. Your waves have changed me from the inside out

II: You showed me love, care, importance
Happiness, positive vibes and just doing best
As much as possible
This is where your waves just took the wheel of my life

III: We did things together and it just felt natural
I started to miss you while going to sleep
I started missing you while at work
I started missing you while going home after seeing you
I started missing your voice all the time
I started to notice little things you would do while you're with me
You really changed my life and I started to rely on you for everything

IV: I did not know what love was until I met you

V: I love your mind more than anything
Excluding your smile
I love your distinct scent
The way you would look at me
The way your magical hands would look and how you'd move them around
I loved when you would ask me to come see you
I love how you would call my name
I love how you would attack me when you would see me
I love how you would try to keep your voice calm around me
I love how you would suggest me diet changes

Youniverse

I love how you would come to me whenever you wanted
I love how you would call me at work to vent
I love how cute you'd look whenever we would go out
I love how you loved getting into my jacket whenever you would feel cold
Sorry
I got carried away with memories

VI: You stopped talking to me for quite some time
And I knew exactly why

VII: I was broken and I missed you so much
Talking to you made everything easy on me
Just hearing your voice made everything bearable

VIII: Believe me when I say I tried my best to move the hell on
But everything and anything I would do
Reminded me of you and your waves
I tried everything in my cookbook to change how I was feeling
I took some time for myself and tried my best
To forget about the past but I ended up reaching out to you

IX: You kept your distance from me
And I noticed that every second I spent with you
It hurt me like no other but it also gave me some warmth
Because no matter what, I was with you at that time
Always felt like a burden for you
I'm sorry

X: Flourish as the flower you are

XI: I will always be here
But I will be gone from your life
But that being said
You will forever stay in my heart and head
I loved you and always will love you like no other
You're not just anyone, Ritu
You can't be forgotten
I'll still come to get your signed copies of your book
You have been a blessing to me

XII: So, thank you for your waves
I'll miss you

— A Letter From An Ex Titled "Ritu Kaur And Her Waves"

Youniverse

The sweet talk that quickly becomes bitter

— *Lies*

Ritu Kaur

*Animals are smarter than us, aren't they?
They don't do things they regret later*

— From Mannu

Youniverse

It's
A
Deep
Pain

An
Intolerable
Pain

A
Pain
With
Many
Pauses
Layers
Lines
Sentences
Chapters
Books
Long

It's
The
Pain
In
Lo(s)ving
You

Ritu Kaur

There is no unit to measure love
But if my love for you could be measured
It would break every scale in the multiverse

— *(Un)cond(it)ional*

Youniverse

Those rooftop bars in New York with you

He had prior relationships before we dated
He dealt with a different type of pain from each one
One of the hardest endings for him
Was probably losing someone to cancer, to death
He lost a love who moved away to a different country
The same love who shortly passed away
Because of cancer
He had to grieve over someone who was
No longer here
Grief over someone he didn't get to say goodbye to
And what about those of us still alive on the planet
At the same time as one another
Am I supposed to believe he's gone
Even though he's out there somewhere
Am I supposed to grieve his loss
Death is a loss that takes time to accept
And sure, this is another type of loss
Which will take time to accept
But I never imagined having to grieve over someone
Still living
I never imagined having to grieve over him
Knowing that he exists out there somewhere
On the same planet as I do
And having to be without him
It's a loss that cuts me deeper
Than the loss of death

Youniverse

To be away from someone you want to be with most
Is a different type of pain
It's a pain that takes away any other feeling
Or logic
It steals your appetite
Sleep and peace
It takes your breath away 'cause the only thing that
Makes you feel like you can breathe again
Is their presence

— *Illusions*

Late autumn
Gloomy weather
FaceTime calls during traffic
Rainy days
Moscato
Random bowling nights
Christmas in New York
Car dates
Boba tea
Petrichor
Late night bars
Dancing in the park at 1am
No curfew

— Reminders Of You

Youniverse

His tongue was my favorite paintbrush

Ritu Kaur

Does it count to have seen you in my dreams?

— *Longing*

Youniverse

You are not just a flower
A plant or a tree
You are the entire garden

— Compliments From Him

Ritu Kaur

Sometimes I close my eyes and imagine you talking softly while you're grazing your fingers through my hair. All while I'm in your embrace. To feel your touch, your warmth, your essence through my imagination once again. It's a soothing memory, until I have to open my eyes again

Youniverse

I feel like you're ingrained in my soul
I truly do
And if that's what love is
Then I'm glad I've loved you

At times it's difficult to write
So I shut my laptop closed
Or put away my pen
'Cause my writing reminds me of you
And that makes it harder to continue
To put the book together
I don't look at it for weeks at a time
Thinking when I go back after a while I'll be fine
But when does it go away
When does it go away
When does the pain go away?
Will it go away when I'm finally done writing about you….
Should I continue?

— Healing Or Hurting? / Hurting To Heal

Youniverse

Everyone tells you that closure will come
But no one talks about how hard it is
To miss someone
'Cause closure is quiet for so long
Closure doesn't operate on human terms
It doesn't tell you who's right or wrong
We mistakenly think we'll get closure from
The other person
But closure is about the peace you've made within
It creeps up on you unexpectedly on its own schedule
According to the youniverse's plan

— What I've Learned About Closure

Ritu Kaur

I wonder if you're going to look back at all this time and remember me someday. And I wonder what you're going to remember about me when you think of me a few years from now, with a mere passage of time, when all of this is over

Youniverse

Do not choose what left you
It was never yours to begin with

Ritu Kaur

Us being together would mean the youniverse would be off balance

Youniverse

Sometimes the only place we can have
In people's lives
Is in their hearts

— *"Unfinished" Love Stories*

Ritu Kaur

Why do we stay in relationships past their expiration dates

Youniverse

Did my hands feel different on you?

Were they initially charming
Are they absent when you need them emotionally
Do they put you down due to their own insecurities
Do they lack empathy
Do they blame you for their own cheating
Do they manipulate you for their own well-being
Do they blackmail you emotionally
Do they blame everyone else
Besides their own flawed reasoning
Do they make you question your sanity
Is there a label on your relationship
Or did they leave you hanging

— Dating A Narcissist I

Youniverse

He broke me in many ways
Not believing he was the first one
Not believing me when I told him I was a victim
Lying to my face saying I was the one he loved
There's more to this
But does this sound familiar
Does this sound like your story
'Cause you're not alone
And if he's called you psycho or crazy
Then you're surely not the crazy one

— *Dating A Narcissist II*

It's difficult to explain emotional abuse
Difficult to show the battle scars for this violence
Difficult to find the words for feelings
Difficult to come to terms with who they are
Difficult to accept myself in the process
Difficult to reach out for help 'cause of judgment
Difficult to reach out for help 'cause no one gets it
Difficult to reach out for help 'cause I'm labelled stupid
Difficult to reach out for help 'cause people
Don't understand what it's like to be with a narcissist
Difficult to express my emotions without others saying
You should leave, why haven't you
You deserve better
You're being stupid
He doesn't love you
It's easy for you to say that
When you're not involved in the abuse
Easy for you to say that the actions shouldn't be accepted
Easy for you to have multiple reasons why I shouldn't stay
Easy for you to come to terms with
When you're not the one in love
Easy for you to dismiss me
When you don't understand my truth
Easy for you to reject my cry for help
'Cause you're tired of going in circles for me
While I'm going through this cycle of abuse
Easy for you to talk about me 'cause you think you know
Easy for you to do all these things
When it isn't you in my shoes

— *Narcissistic Abuse*

Youniverse

And when you say we're done
Why do you wait a week or two
To return

April 7, 2018. It's 2:40am: I can't breathe. I woke up from a deep sleep around 2am. I went to my siblings and woke them up 'cause I didn't know what to do. This was the last time I slept in my room.

April 8, 2018. It's 1:32am: Cannot sleep. Staring at the ceiling, trying to breathe. Today's the first day I switch rooms for Dev. I thought with Mannu and Anshi being here I'd feel safer but I feel like no one can hear me. I feel really bad whenever I wake them up because I can't breathe. I don't know why I'm feeling this way, it's bothering me.

April 9, 2018. It's 4:34am: Almost fell asleep but I got up to open up the blinds, room windows and turn on the lights. I got so anxious I was going to cry. Mannu and Anshi are disturbed by me again. They aren't upset, they want to make sure I'm okay.

April 10, 2018. It's 4:48am: Everyone's snoring seems to be so much louder. My white noise app is no longer helping me like it used to, even though I try to keep it close to my ear to block out all of the noise; my ears are sensitive and pick up Anshi's breathing even though she's not sharing a bed with me. I'm so anxious I want to get out of the house and scream. I can't breathe. I feel blind looking into the room because I don't have my contacts in. I'm scared. It's really dark.

April 11, 2018. It's 2:55am: I didn't take out my contact lenses tonight because I get extremely anxious when I feel blind in this room. I have trouble sleeping tonight due to everyone snoring. I actually feel slightly better since I don't feel as anxious. I opened the window for air and turned on the closet light. *Maybe it was a few days thing.* Trying to be positive and hopeful. Maybe today's the last time I will be documenting this.

April 12, 2018. It's 3:18am: Contact lenses are still in my eyes. I've noticed small things trigger me and cause anxiety but they're all irrelevant and illogical. It makes me wonder what I've suppressed. Like my co-workers sharing stories with me or Mummy Ji telling me something random about herself. Just now I opened the Tumblr app, and without anything being loaded yet I had instant anxiety. Opened up Instagram and immediately closed it before seeing a single post. Feeling that since I'm experiencing a high level of anxiety, my mind can't hear, see or experience anything else that can worsen it. Even though the content I see makes no sense as to why I would be triggered? I'm a bit concerned because this has never happened before.

April 13, 2018. It's 4:12am: Contact lenses have been in for three nights and are bothering me but I can't deal with anymore anxiety attacks. I've had three hours of sleep in the last week. I've become irritated with everyone snoring. I said "Anshi, there are several reasons as to why I can't sleep but your snoring happens to be one of them." I feel terrible because she woke up right away. Mannu surprisingly didn't. I want to cry. I have sensory overload. I fell asleep for a very short time but since I haven't been sleeping, I immediately had a vivid dream. In my dream I was trying to protect a younger girl so I started fighting a woman, who happened to be very strong but so was I. I ended up on top of the woman, choking her with my legs. I could feel her suffocating and I stopped choking her after noticing she was going to die. In my dream I was trying to let this woman know not to bother me. I woke up right away

after letting her free. I turned on all of the lights.
Opened the windows. Went to mom finally. Told her
about all of this and she told me I need to go to the
doctor. Mummy Ji hugged me and now I feel like
crying. I can't believe I felt someone physically
suffocating in a dream. I saw the woman's eyes roll
back; I still remember everything vividly, it's
disturbing. I felt like I was suffocating in real life as I
was choking the woman, which caused me to wake
up. I was out of breath. I know dreams aren't literal
but the fact that I almost killed someone in a dream
state gives me great anxiety because I could never
consciously make a decision like that in reality. It felt
so real. Still trying to process it. My heart feels
heavy. I'm actually crying 'cause I can't do this. And
I don't know what I'm doing wrong. I haven't been
eating much because I don't have an appetite. I
finally felt hungry after hanging with some friends
and ended up ordering takeout. I felt happy that my
stomach growled. It's been empty but lately I get sick
thinking of eating or drinking anything, including
water. I drink water in small sips to keep myself
hydrated. I can only drink it normally at the gym.
And that's the other thing. I've been doing quick
workouts because I'm low on energy since I haven't
been eating, but I still want to go to keep myself
motivated, in shape and to help with the anxiety.
Doesn't seem like it's working. Possibly need a
nightlight and an oxygen mask. I am so exhausted, I
can't focus. I have terrible memory. I'm not mindful.
I am irritable even though I try to control it 'cause I
don't want to feel irritated. It bothers me to feel this
way when I know irritation wouldn't be my normal
reaction to most things. I'm much more clumsy, I've
been dropping my phone more often, causing the
phone screen to crack each time. Mood fluctuations,
sensory overload. So, so tired, I wish I could sleep.

It's 3:57pm: I'm sitting at a stoplight. Anxious.

January 23, 2019. It's 2:22am: I thought I'd never come back to log anything again. Felt like it was redundant and that there was no point but my heart is heavy tonight with reminders of you. I miss you like crazy. I don't know why I'm longing for you again. It's almost been a year since you became someone else's. I thought the hurt would leave by now.

January 26, 2019. It's 9:10pm: I've been sleeping on my parents' bed 'cause they're back home in the motherland for two months. I can't help but cry because I miss you so much and there is nothing I can do. I've noticed that my sense of smell has weakened in the last three months. I didn't notice it till recently, but that's because I remembered all of the times I couldn't smell something others were talking about; I thought it was because my nose had some blockages, but it turns out that my sense of smell is very different now. Maybe that's why I rarely have an appetite. I'm at my lowest weight since my first year of college, in 2011. That scares me because I wonder what else I haven't noticed about myself since going through grief this past year.

February 5, 2019. It's 7:46pm: I woke up from heart palpitations again. They were scary. Ever since I stopped using Mary Jane I've been having vivid dreams of you. Dreams that feel so real they seem like they took place somewhere else. I miss you deeply. Today I got confirmation that maybe you did really love me at some point. And it hurts how I noticed it in such a small way. How people treat you when it comes to food and time. With you there was never a no to food; whenever I asked you where we were going to eat next, you'd tell me to choose. With you there was no limit with time. We could talk for hours and still not be tired of each other. Today I hung out with a couple of guy friends who didn't care to eat and wanted to leave after one activity. I wanted to leave too. I don't expect chemistry with everyone I come across, even old and new acquaintances. But that's not the point. The point is with you, there was everything. A friend. A lover. A safe space. You were one of a kind, darling. I'll remember the laughs more than the pain.

February 6, 2019. It's 3:21am: I can't sleep and I'm longing for you. All I want in this moment is to be held by you. I wonder if you're alive. Everything seems fabricated. I wonder if I really knew you. If I really met you. If our memories are real. I find myself trying to delete our pictures and videos but I end up looking through them instead. My heart feels like it's going to come out of my chest.

It's 12:22pm: My boss just told me my attendance and punctuality to work has been inconsistent since I started working here three months ago. This is the third time I've been in her office regarding my absences and tardiness. She stated she understands my health isn't the greatest but that I can't allow it to interfere with my work. She says she gets it. That she's been through it before and that I need to do something to ease my physical symptoms, whether it's pain medication or keeping the nausea under control. But everything she says goes through one ear and out the other. Heartbreak isn't a solid reason for missing work, but when heartbreak impacts your mental and physical states, when it's the reason behind most of your pain, nothing anyone says matters. Nothing anyone says seems to help. Nothing anyone says seems genuine. Nothing anyone says makes them seem like they truly understand. That's how I'm feeling. Except I feel like I'm the wall 'cause nothing is getting through to me.

February 7, 2019. It's 2:37am: The thought of you sickens me tonight. It disgusts me, frankly. The amount of times you were unfaithful to me. The amount of times you lied to me. The amount of times you hurt me, and I forgave you every single time. You weren't my first love, but you were the one I had a lot of firsts with. You were someone who had a lot of experience with relationships while I barely had any. Maybe to you it wasn't special, but I gave you my all. Everything. I shattered myself loving you. So why do I still think about you? Why do I still love you?

It's 12:52pm: I'm at the creek on my lunch break. The flowers are starting to bloom again. The field is covered in green. I miss you. I'm wearing my glasses today because my eyes have become too sensitive to wear contact lenses. But one of my coworker's told me I look like a 'hot teacher' so there's that. I miss you. I hate that I miss you. I hate that I can't do anything about it. I hate that you've hurt me and I still feel like I'm the one who took a loss.

February 11, 2019. It's 9:37am: Today I'm wearing the waves Pandora bracelet and 'R' lettered necklace you gifted me that Christmas. Just to have the weight of you on me. Just to feel something on my body that was picked out by you. Touched by you.

February 15, 2019. It's 1:35pm: I'm at the creek again. It's pouring. I'm feeling nauseous. I'm worried about my health. I've been having random pain, headaches and symptoms but I can't keep calling in to work. I can't afford to. You wished me happy Valentine's Day yesterday. I saw your message and became numb. I didn't process it right away. It felt like I had imagined your message. I missed you so much. I still do. I didn't reply. My heart woke me up last night. It feels like someone else is on the bed. Maybe I'm crazy. But my heartbeat has become so rapid and strong that I end up waking up from heart palpitations several times each night.

March 5, 2019. It's 6:55am: My parents are back from the motherland. I quit my job at the funeral home a few days ago. Yesterday my mother asked me if I've heard from you recently. I was thinking about you so her question caught me off guard. I told her I haven't, that you've moved on. She smiled peacefully, said that's good, that you and your wife are probably going to be pregnant in another six months. Of course I've thought of you having kids with her but not to this extent. I've been thinking about what my mother said since yesterday. It hurts. It hurts so much.

March 26, 2019. It's 10:16am: It's my cousin's wedding week. It'll be the first real wedding I'll ever attend. I can't help but think of how you went through it when it was your time, from the male perspective. You got married sometime a year ago. Said it should've been me in her place. Told me you never cried as much as you did the night before your wedding; and you wanted to see me afterwards 'cause you couldn't forget about me. You broke my heart you broke my heart you broke my heart.

March 28, 2019. It's 4:08am: My cousin showed me her wedding dress since I can't make it as I'm taking the LSAT the same day. She showed me the lingerie for when she goes to his house that night. My heart dropped. My stomach turned. It instantly made me think of you, your wife. How your wife was planning this during her time. How you were planning this during your time. I'm reliving the feelings of betrayal, rejection, heartbreak, the hurt. This time more vividly through my cousin's marriage. Everyone keeps saying I'm next. But I can't even think about loving anyone again, let alone trusting anyone again. I can't imagine myself going through any of this. Because I pictured it with you but that ship sailed long ago. I wish I could stop thinking about all of this. How dare you say I never cared. I'm shattered. I wish I could wipe you from my memory.

April 10, 2019. It's 1:17pm: The train just stopped at Embarcadero station. I looked up from my phone when I noticed the doors remained open for a while. Saw the E when I stretched to look outside. This is your stop. And it's a special day. It feels like this is my moment to get out and come see you at work. Normally I would've had circumstances been different. But I don't know of your whereabouts and I don't want to know of your whereabouts. I hope you're well. The doors to the train have closed.

April 13, 2019. It's 9:15am: You emailed me the day after your birthday. To both of my emails. To ensure that I'd get your 10-page letter. I wasn't aware of the letter till this morning and my heart was racing the entire time I read it. Your letter was a response to one of my private blog posts about you. And it hurts so much that you don't know about how much I've loved you and how much you've hurt me. So you say things like I never cared. That I lied to you. That I never had regard for your feelings. Life hurts without you but it hurts more with you in it.

April 15, 2019. It's 3:15pm: I'm trying to continue to put the book together but I feel zero motivation. I'm deeply depressed. I miss you so much I'm crying. Life feels broken. I want to be over you already. Why is it so difficult to get you out of my head?

It's 5:26pm: I needed a drive. The clouds and I have something in common. We're both releasing water. The rain is hitting the windshield and it reminds me of all the car dates we had together in the rain. When we'd get take out, when we'd cuddle, when we'd talk about random things for hours. You have no idea how much I miss you.

April 17, 2019. It's 5:21am: I'm truly sorry for all of the pain I've caused you. It hurts to know that I've hurt you.

June 9, 2019. It's 4:50pm: It's warm out today. It reminds me of you.

July 17, 2019. It's 1:08am: I miss you. I've been missing you. You're still my favorite song. It's been difficult to write. I can't remember the last time I did. I've been putting it off and I'm supposed to be working on this book. Thoughts of you still hurt and I think of you every single day, doesn't matter how I feel or what I'm doing, you still come to my mind daily. You're a regular visitor without warning. I wish I could ban you from my mind but that would mean I'm not human. I hope you're well and I've come to terms with you being a narcissist. How you'd do things "for me" 'cause ultimately they benefited you in some way. How you counted what you did for me. How you weren't there when I needed you emotionally, which is the most important thing to me. Thinking of everything that happened between us for the time that we were together. The "good," the bad, the ugly. Knowing that your actions were inauthentic. Does that make it better or worse?

August 1, 2019. It's 1:41am: I remember you thinking I was bipolar and psychotic just because I'd get distant from you. You knew why I would but you thought it was me being crazy, bipolar or psychotic just like you claimed your exes to be. I wonder if that's another case of projection. It hurts that you think this way but it reminds me that I never knew you or your actual thoughts. You kept your true feelings hidden away so all I can assume at this point is you thinking the worst of me and making me think about all of my flaws. You brought out the worst in me, that's the saddest thing. You misunderstood me, you made me feel ugly, you made me second guess myself, you'd gaslight me, you'd lie to me, you never chose me, you'd bring up excuses as to why we couldn't be and once it was "too late" you said you didn't know what to do. You tossed me out and said I did that to you. Why was I the one who got left and the one the finger points to? 'Cause I tried for you. I begged you. I went to your sister. I asked to meet your parents. I said I'd do anything to make it right with you. But that wasn't enough for you. I wasn't enough for you. You made me question myself for months and a couple of years and even now I still do sometimes. I wonder if I'm doing the right thing, being myself, doing what makes me happy. I always try to ensure that I am. I'm glad I don't conform to other people's ideas of love, acceptance and social status. It didn't used to feel like it but now I know that being apart from you is one right thing for me.

Ritu Kaur

August 19, 2019. It's 2:31pm: *Do you still think about him?* Anshi just asked me this question and I asked her who she was referring to. She rolled her eyes because she knows I know. She said I don't speak of you anymore. I still think about you everyday. I dreamt of you last night. But what good does it do to talk about you? To keep you alive by talking about you. You come to my mind everyday, and sometimes I still let you sleep over. That's why you show up in my dreams.

August 22, 2019. It's 12:17am: I miss you tonight. But it's not a longing type of miss. It's a different type of miss— one where I'm living my life and hoping you're living yours too. I just started reading your old letters and emails for familiarity. For comfort. It's easier some days than others but the pain has left for the most part. I still think of you each day out of habit, but I know with time that will fade too. I can sleep in the dark without the white noise now. I take out my contact lenses every night. I'm doing better, feeling better, eating better, I've even gained some weight in the last couple of months.

September 15, 2019. It's 2:05am: Life is fragile. We're meant to learn through our experiences and those lessons are meant to humble us. We change each day without seeing it but one day your life is one thing and the next day it can be completely different. That's how it feels when I think of you. All of the patterns. Red flags. Things I ignored. When I didn't listen to my intuition. I thought my reality was one thing based on what you were telling me. But this is how you were meant to reach me. To teach me. Through pain. Damaging pain. And my oh my have I learned a thing or two from you. I forgive you for everything. I forgive myself for not trusting myself, for blaming myself. I've found forgiveness, I've found peace. I'm weeping but it's a dull sadness. A sadness that feels like it's hiding somewhere even when life is good. Maybe that's just a part of being human, knowing that it is both joy and pain that help us ascend. And ultimately I thank you for being a lesson because at the end of the day, this is all temporary. You. Me. The pain. This vessel. This life. This time of existence. It's bittersweet but earth is all about duality, right? It feels refreshing to move on.

September 18, 2019. It's 9:22am: I found safety in your arms a long time ago. Life is strange in that way. You felt warm but were you? Was it my warmth that I spread to you? I remember when I was sick; the pain, the nausea, the endless symptoms I felt yet doctors could find nothing. Having tubes put through my body yet I was still told that I was normal. I wonder how many doctors thought I was a hypochondriac. I've read about how being with a narcissist can make you sick because you put them above yourself for every matter, you do everything for them and you're unaware of how it starts to kill you inside. But you start feeling sick and not knowing why. It's why I couldn't finish my meals when you were in my life. But that was a different time. Reflecting on that time makes me sad mostly for losing my innocence. I thought people were good and honest. You showed me that isn't always the case. So many things still trigger me but I try to get through them. Life constantly reminds me that everything, everything is temporary. Even the safety I once found in your arms.

It's 5:13pm: I remember when you saw me after months you said I looked bony. I stopped seeing you for some time. A couple of months went by and you asked to see me again. This time you said my cheeks had gotten chubby. You knew I'd overthink your subtle messages and let them destroy me. That's what you wanted to do. Any chance that you got you had to make sure I questioned myself, any chance you got you put me down. I did everything I could to make you happy but nothing was enough for you. You were an endless hole sucking everything from me and I destroyed myself loving you. But destroying myself had to happen in this life, just so I could learn how to put myself together.

You used to excuse your friends' cheating and stated women shouldn't be doing the same. You told me about your friend's five-year relationship and how he was also talking to someone else. I told you that wasn't right for him to do; you stated the woman that he was cheating with wasn't a "nice girl." I asked you what that made your friend out to be since he was the one cheating in the relationship. But like society, you blamed the woman instead of the man who went out there to be unfaithful. You said that "girl" didn't have a good reputation and I asked you how you knew. You said your friend had told you. I asked you why you believed him if you had never spoken to the woman but you stayed silent. Moments afterwards you said that I was right. That you shouldn't have judged her 'cause you don't know the truth. What lies did you spread about me? How many times did you say I wasn't a "nice girl?" Or that I was crazy or had issues. I was taught that when people gossip with you, they gossip about you. Nevertheless, your deluded opinions no longer bother me. You lost that power a long time ago.

Youniverse

September 25, 2019. It's 10:36pm: My brother turned 25 yesterday. Seeing Mannu come home to his little surprise was heartwarming— he's always appreciative. Anshi, Mannu and I went to the movies together. It was nice to go out to the movies after a long time. I kept trying to think of my brother not growing up, I felt sad throughout the day thinking of how we all grow older. Like when I was 25 a couple of years ago, I published my first book. And I'm going to be 27 soon. 13 years ago I was 14. In another 13 years I'll be 40. I miss my mom. I miss my mom even though she's here. I miss her even though she's in the room next to me. She feels far away. I miss her so much. I just had a breakdown and Mummy Ji told me to choose happiness. She said that life is short, but how many times do I have to hear that? How many times will something or someone else besides my thoughts tell me that? Of course everything is temporary. What would be the point if it wasn't? Time is a social construct. But aren't we time ourselves? Constantly aging and getting closer to death with each moment that passes before we do— yet we live acting like the next moment is promised. We overestimate the wrong things.

September 26, 2019. It's 4:51pm: I'm grateful I broke out of the cycle. I'm thankful to the youniverse that we never got married. I've read multiple articles and blogs that talk about narcissistic abuse, recovery, narcissistic victim syndrome and how people just don't understand this unless they've actually been in the situation. During the time we dated, I thought seeing you made things better. I was dying internally being with you, not knowing the causes of being unwell, irritable, unhappy most of the time. You treated me like a drug. You took me in doses. Some days left me emptier than others. You said I was your

Ritu Kaur

drug, I hated that. I'm not a drug, I'm not a vacation. I'm a person, a home, someone with feelings, needs and dreams of my own. How dare you. How dare you lessen me to something to fulfill your needs, your emptiness, your selfishness. I'm still recovering, still trying to fully release these deeper feelings that I keep to myself.

It's 11:26pm: I used to be so fond of you. I put you on a pedestal and thought you exceeded my expectations. I should've known you were too good to be true. I've read more forums about narcissistic personality disorder, narcissistic victim syndrome, questions about physical symptoms that people have experienced (anhedonia being one of several); questions about if narcissists can truly love, how long it takes to heal from this form of abuse, how it feels like it's difficult to trust or see yourself in a relationship after this, how long I should wait before I date again, how victims experience C-PTSD (Complex Post-Traumatic Stress Disorder) afterwards. I read about all of these things to make sure that I'm not crazy. That there are others out there who wonder about the same things I do, those who wondered about this years ago when they went through it, so I know I'm not alone. I know I'm not making this up. I know what I went through was abusive but I never knew it was to this extent. Thank you for teaching me; I feel far away from myself but there's no going back. I'm a different person, I'm learning to unlearn you, the habits you instilled in me, and who I was.

October 5, 2019. It's 4:44am: I remember when you asked me if I thought you loved me. I told you that you didn't. I still remember exactly how your face dropped and turned red. You kept trying to prove

Youniverse

through words how much you "loved" me. You said you treated me like a gem. How come I didn't shine like one when I was with you?

October 9, 2019. It's 12:34pm: I'm sitting in a hospital room with Mummy Ji, with our fingers intertwined. *Youniverse* is going to be published tomorrow. I still feel the pain of your absence here and there. But I can breathe. I never realized that grief could cause this much pain and anxiety. Thank you for the lessons. I needed you in this life. To be who I am. But farewell old love, I hope you're happy. Maybe somewhere down the line, in five decades or so, we'll accidentally bump into each other and laugh at all of the pain we caused. Perhaps that'll be our final farewell. But until then or not, goodbye and take care.

October 10, 2019. It's 4:44am: We used to be out at this time. It's weird to me how I've been going to work at this time for the past few months— it reminds me of the times we used to grab food at this hour, or go on an adventure or just talk and fall asleep. These hours make it seem like life is truly fabricated. It's quiet. Peaceful. A bit melancholic. But mostly quiet.

— How Long It Took Me To Grieve Your "Death" / Anxiety Attack Log / Narcissistic Victim Syndrome

Ritu Kaur

Jehra koyi sache piaar naal dhokha kar da eh
Oho kadhi sukhi nehi rehnda

Translation:
The one who betrays a lover
Whom has loved them unconditionally
Does not get peace

— *From Mummy Ji*

Youniverse

We're here to fulfill soul contracts
They're meant to awaken us and push us on our path
They may not always teach us in the most tender of ways
Some come gently
But all experiences and teachers are different
Just like in school
There were some teachers we liked, disliked, loved
The relationships around us are meant to enhance our growth
Despite how painful
Ascension requires letting go of attachment

Ritu Kaur

Sometimes anxiety and toxic feelings are a way
For your body to warn you it's rejecting a person

Youniverse

Maybe I chose to come into this life
Without my soul mate
Is this why I'm perfectly content
In solitude

Ritu Kaur

You cannot live through another person

Youniverse

This is your reminder that impermanence
Is the only constant in life

Ritu Kaur

We have five fingers on our hands
Just like people
They are all different

— *What My Mother Taught Me*

Youniverse

We can learn tremendously from trees
They're silent storytellers

Ritu Kaur

We become consumed with what the youniverse has taken away from us that we tend to miss what it's creating for us

Youniverse

I allow the waves to push me
To shove me
To drown me for a bit
Just so I can let the ocean know
I have listened
I have seen
I have understood
That each wave I have felt
Has taught me to rise above
Even if I cannot swim
I can learn how
Even if I'm going in the opposite direction
I can learn to flow
As long as I don't force

Ritu Kaur

I lost inches off my waist from the depression
From the anxiety
From the stress
When people would tell me I looked better
I wanted to tell them I didn't feel better
When people asked me what diet I was on
I replied with depression
Most of them would laugh and ask, *no but really*
What are you doing?
You've become thin
It's the depression
It's the heartbreak
It's the loss of appetite 'cause nothing appeals to you
People think you're starving yourself
Or taking appetite suppressant pills
Or hard drugs
Or altering your body through plastic procedures
But what do you do when anxiety fills you up
When depression numbs your appetite
When your body no longer feels right
You get told you look the greatest you ever have
While feeling like the exact opposite
Am I more appealing 'cause I lost inches off my waist?
Am I more appealing 'cause I take up less space?
What is it about me that makes you feel this way?
'Cause I don't feel okay

Youniverse

Familial ties
Relationships
Friendships
All end when we outgrow others
When we no longer vibe on the same frequency as others
So when we are trying our best to save
Any type of relationship which is damaged
Beyond repair
We are going against the natural process of death
By providing light to dead ends while ignoring the rosebud that is waiting to bloom right next to us
Or across from us
We are going against the normal process of letting go
By watering dead flowers
Instead of letting the petals decompose into the soil
We are so focused on staying or having someone stay
That we allow the thorn to continually poke us
Over and over
Leave us bleeding if it means we'll get to hold it just a bit longer
All while ignoring the growth of another rose
Another relationship
That is ready for us
Only if we are also ready for it

— *The Rosebud Isn't Another Person*

Ritu Kaur

Do you also weep when you write?

Youniverse

The bad moments only turn into
Bad days
When we don't leave them
As they are

Ritu Kaur

We break our own hearts whenever we confuse
teachers for soul mates

Youniverse

Farewells are often needed
But only occasionally given

— Why?

I thought about suicide several times before I found my purpose
But since I've found my purpose
I know that I can't leave until I fulfill my mission
I might have a bad day today
I might not want to be here
I might not want to live
But that's okay
'Cause tomorrow is another day and tomorrow I'll want to live
And even if not tomorrow
There's the day after that and after that and after that….

I don't know what it was about Kern's mango juice
That made life seem like everything would be okay
I looked forward to drinking Kern's mango juice
Whenever I came home from school
Whenever I ate a slice of pizza
Or whenever Mummy Ji would make roti
I drank Kern's mango juice for years
The carton juice box that makes me feel nostalgic for the 90s
I drank Kern's mango juice until I got sick of it
Sick of the sugar
Sick of the artificial flavor
Sick of the yellow color
That I looked forward to pouring in a glass
What was it about Kern's mango juice
That I could no longer stand
It's almost been two decades since I last got a taste
I still remember its scent and flavor
How it was a time that I genuinely embraced
How each stage in our lives
Is merely a phase
Just like Kern's mango juice and its once sweet taste

The birds remind me of you
You make the home complete when you're here
I haven't seen the birds since you went to visit the motherland
I thought it was because it had been raining recently
That they haven't visited or eaten the rice we laid out for them
Today I put out lentils and seeds for them
Thinking that the different colors of food may attract them
Changed their water and awaited their arrival for 9am
No presence
No Motu Papa
No Blue Jay
No tiny baby birds that Motu Papa birthed
No other gang of birds that rival with Blue Jay
I'm still sitting here two hours later
Since the birds come at 9am, 11am, 3pm and 6pm
It's now 11:07am and they're still not here
The backyard is empty without their presence
I'm trying to hold in my tears but they can't be stopped today
I told you that the birds miss you
Oh really, how do you know?
You asked me with an innocent laugh
I just know, I told you
You give them gourmet meals and options, Mummy
You started laughing again and said
Yeah they're spoiled now, but they come and go
Just like us, I thought
But do the birds feels your absence too, Mata?
Is that why they haven't returned?

— *Grief*

Youniverse

The things my mother does that make me smile
She hides snacks where she makes roti
But if we find them
She says they're ours, that she didn't want them
We tease her saying she purposely hid them and she
Starts smiling
When she's tired but still asks us what we want to eat
How she squeals in laughter when she tries to share a funny story
The way her eyes look when she wakes up in the morning
Mom, Mummy Ji, Mata Sri
She used to say *you'll never find a mother like me*
I would believe it even if she never told me

Ritu Kaur

We don't remember everyone who was temporary

Youniverse

I've never had a big home
Only a big heart
Which people tend to make
A home out of

Ritu Kaur

You are here simply because
The youniverse decided
It needed your existence

Youniverse

My mother told me
The way we think is also a karmic debt
That I should be proud of my level of consciousness

Ritu Kaur

Going through tough times
Doesn't dim your light
You're just as radiant
As you've always been

Youniverse

We are taught to hate and hate and hate
We tremble at the smallest sign of tenderness

You called today
The number on my screen looked familiar
Still, I hesitated to answer but I did anyway
Thinking it may have been an appointment reminder
I wasn't surprised to hear your voice on the other end
But I couldn't recall unblocking your phone number
You were asking for my birthday
You confused mine with Mannu's
I was unsure if I should correct you
I was still trying to remember when I deleted you
Off of my block list
Then you stated Dev's birthday and Anshi's
You asked me for mine
Confirmed the dates of our birth
You asked if I could send them to you in a message
I asked you why you needed them
Just 'cause, you replied
Just wanted to keep them
I realized your call came through
'Cause I had gotten a new phone
I knew exactly where to enter it when we hung up

— *He Doesn't Know The Age Of His Children / June 28, 2018*

Youniverse

You don't always have to burn the bridge
You can build one over them

Ritu Kaur

On days when I am longing for my mother
I sit next to her asking her to braid my hair
Something I didn't look forward to as a kid
'Cause I despised being teased for having a long braid
It's funny how we learn to embrace the things we hated as kids
'Cause that time won't come back and we know this
When I am longing for my mother and don't know what to say
I lay next to her asking her if she wants to play a game of *Sorry*
She's the green pawn, I'm blue
Sometimes we secretly let each other win
Sometimes we tease each other when the other is losing
I see the inner-child in my mother daily
When I am longing for my mother's presence
And she isn't here
I feel a deep sense of yearning
Like I'll never have enough time
But she's the one I want to be with most
So I consider this a crime
When I am longing for my mother's warmth
I embrace her in a hug while we watch the birds
The birds she feeds each day 'cause that's her way
Of spreading love
When I am longing for my mother
I cry
I cry
I cry
'Cause I will never know about all of the pain she feels inside
When I am longing for my mother I thank the youniverse
For blessing me with a soul as pure as hers

Youniverse

They look for god everywhere
I see her in my mother

Ritu Kaur

She's feisty, she's fierce
She interrogates me for jokes
Her meals are cooked with the right amount of spices, overdosed with love
She comes with smarts and deep thoughts
Her eyes twinkle like the stars
Her laugh echoes throughout our home
Anshi is one of the most beautiful souls I've ever known

Youniverse

How much knowledge do we lose when someone passes?

We say things like the ocean is wild
But not alive
Or
The fire is burning but not living
But who are we to say that they aren't alive
Is it 'cause fire doesn't breathe the way we want it to
Fire can burn people to death
The ocean can swallow us whole
Does that make these elements murderers
Or just Mother Nature taking its course
How are these things not considered to be alive
If they're doing what they're meant to do

Youniverse

Oftentimes this life still feels foreign to me

— *From Someplace Else*

Ritu Kaur

Control your thoughts
Your thoughts become
Your life

— *Universal Truth*

Youniverse

My heart hurts
From the hurt others have experienced

— *Empath*

I came across a video today
That loneliness is twice as deadly as obesity
And as deadly as smoking a pack of cigarettes a day
But most of us still suffer from loneliness
Even though we live in the most connected age
We are the most disconnected
Loneliness makes you hate people
Distrust people
It makes you think the worst of people
And most of us isolate ourselves from everyone once
we've been hurt by humans far too many times
Then we have PTSD and don't read social cues
correctly
We assume people don't have pure intentions
We isolate ourselves more
Feeling alone and cold in the world
Coming off as cold to others, when we aren't
And it just becomes an endless cycle
Of loneliness
Of depression
Of loneliness
Of loneliness
Of loneliness

Youniverse

When I tell you that I feel ugly
I am not waiting for you to tell me that I'm beautiful
When I tell you that I don't feel my best
I don't want you to tell me that I'm perfect
'Cause it's not about your feelings towards me
It's about my feelings towards myself
And how beauty isn't the answer I'm looking for
I want to sit in my ugly feelings for a while
Embrace them
Then let them go once I'm done listening to them
Maybe I feel ugly 'cause I had a long day
Maybe I feel ugly 'cause someone else made me feel that way
Maybe I feel ugly without reason
So when I tell you that I feel ugly
And your response has to do with how
Sexually appealing you "still" find me to be
You're not doing me a favor
You're contributing to the patriarchal standards
That made me feel ugly in the first place

Ritu Kaur

Accountability is responsibility

— *Not Blame Or Fault*

Youniverse

People.
When they're not in the situation
Yet somehow always have the most to say

— *Outsiders*

Ritu Kaur

They asked
Aren't you afraid of working here?

She answered
Afraid of who? The dead? Or the living?

— *Working At A Mortuary*

Youniverse

Do you know how long it's taken for me to accept my body. Accept. Not love. Accept. I'm learning to love my body, but for now I have accepted it. How must my body feel. Over the course of two and a half decades. It is two and a half decades later that I'm embracing this vessel that I'm in. It is over two decades later that I'm experiencing self-acceptance in regards to my physical appearance. My body has waited over two decades for this moment. Twenty something years. Some people wait their entire lives. Some people never get there. Where are you?

Ritu Kaur

There is already enough pain in the world
You'd think we'd be kinder to each other

Youniverse

You cannot acknowledge the light within me
Until you acknowledge the light within yourself

Ritu Kaur

Consciousness is not limited to the brain

Youniverse

They let you see them in the nude
Before letting you see them naked

What breaks me deeply about
This patriarchal world
Is that it is men who have made it this way
And it is men
Who suffer just as much as we do as women
In their own ways
In their own struggles
Well men can't be raped
I looked at him to ensure I heard him correctly
Men can't be raped
He repeated it with a soft chuckle this time
My stomach turned
I felt sick to the bone
It is natural as a woman to talk about my emotions
Men bury their feelings so deep into their chest
It's almost as if their feelings are nonexistent
Then we wonder why we have generations of
Abuse
We wonder why we have generations of
Bloodshed
We wonder why we have generations of
Silence
Yes, it is men who have made the world this way
And it is men who suffer just as much

— *The Suffering We Don't Talk About*

Youniverse

We praise men when their wives birth sons
We shun women when they birth daughters

— *The Violence In Double Standards*

Ritu Kaur

I'm not marriage material
I won't work it out if you cheat
If you were able to stray so easily
Why should I have to question my worth
Or suffer silently
I'm not submissive
That doesn't mean I'm aggressive or inconsiderate
But it does mean that we're equal
What I say is just as important as what you say
So maybe these things scare men away
Scare families away
Scare conformists away
But if equality scares you away
My existence will too

— *Not Your Traditional Marriage Material*

Youniverse

Internalized misogyny is self-hatred

Ritu Kaur

Capitalism is a form of violence

Youniverse

Why do we spend more time with our co-workers
Than our families

— 8+Hour Work Days Are Not Normal, Just Tolerated

Ritu Kaur

The illusion of choice

— *Demockracy*

Youniverse

We make the world run
But do we run the world

— *The 99%*

Ritu Kaur

People don't want to see black on anything but clothes

Youniverse

True activism isn't based on being likable
True activism isn't focused on seeming more
enlightened than others
True activism isn't invalidating social issues
That do not relate to you
Activism
Not true activism
Activism
Which if true in the first place
Is passionate
It's ugly
It's exhausting
It's hopeful
It's resilient
It's revolutionary
Activism is standing up for an issue
Even if it means losing people in the process
Activism is educating others to work towards a
revolution
Even if it means you won't get to see those changes
In your lifetime
Activism is standing up for an issue
Even if you have to stand for it alone

— *To My Revolutionaries In Each Form*

Ritu Kaur

Your fragile feelings are not important to us when you choose to be selectively sympathetic towards atrocities against a group of people based on their geographical location

— *White Feelings*

Youniverse

If Africa is the heart
While Asia and Australia are the lungs
We need both to survive
We need both to be present
If Morocco is the vein connecting the heart to the
ring finger
And Mexico is the spine that helps us move
We require both to live
We require both to groove
If Turkey is my left eye
And Indonesia is my right
I need both eyes to see
I need both eyes for sight
If Punjab are the very feet beneath me on this journey
And Tonga and Peru are the shoulders carrying the
strength for me
If the blood in my veins is not different from yours
What makes us think anyone is more important than
the other?
If Antarctica is the heart
And North and South America are the lungs
We're all the same
We all come from one

Ritu Kaur

If religion was taught correctly
We'd have a generation of thinkers
But it's taught to be used as a weapon
To instill fear in others
Teachings have been lost through centuries of translation
Each faith was meant to teach us that
Love is the foundation

Youniverse

Dictated by identity

— *Prisoner*

Ritu Kaur

When you call me a savage
Is it because I am one with nature
When you call me a savage
Is it because I live like an "animal"
Is it because I share
Is it because I respect the Earth I live on
The Indigenous people
The ones referred to as primitive people
Or as savages
The ones who live with the least tangible things
The ones who know that there is a mission
To spread love and light while we inhabit Earth
What deeds have they done to be deemed as such?
As savages
If this is what it means to be a savage then consider me one
'Cause a savage respects Earth
A savage shares with others
A savage coexists with nature

Youniverse

My pen is my sword
My voice is my weapon
My existence will make you feel empowered
Or intimidated

— Choices

Maybe we haven't had it all
But at least we've had each other through it all

— *Family*

Youniverse

I'm 5'7 and weigh 148 pounds when I walk in
I've had six tests done
Doc still hasn't determined what's "wrong" with me
I wait over an hour in his office until he finally pops in
I inform him I'm still unwell
I tell him I don't have an appetite
That I know my body
That the nausea is impacting my quality of life
How much do you weigh?
His question catches me off guard
I'm 5'7 and weigh 148 pounds when I walk into his office
And that's exactly what I tell him
You shouldn't weigh that much, you should be 130 pounds
*Lose weight and you **may** decrease your symptoms*
I feel more nauseous
I feel more sick
I feel lightheaded
I close my eyes to take a deep breath in
Let it out
I leave the office without another word
I try different doctors but they make me go in circles
Now I'm worried I may have an undetected form of cancer
Losing inches off my waist without trying
Suffering from insomnia, mood swings, I'm crying
No one's able to tell me what's wrong
Yet they make me sit hours in the waiting room or in the ER
Just to say *everything's clear, you're good to go*
But everything's not clear that's why I showed up
No one's taking me seriously, is it all in my head?
Or is ignoring patients' concerns a part of the hellthcare plan?

To ensure that a business stems from a foundation of diseases
Where patients are treated like customers, not human beings
Where insurance determines what kind of care we get
How insurance requires authorization before providing services
Hell I worked in orthopedics I know how it works
All dependent on our level of income
They say it's a part of the policy
If you can't afford services that's not their problem
Yet people are put in asylums for trying to kill themselves
So if I attempt suicide they'll try to keep me alive
But if I go in for an office visit they don't care if I'm dying
Do you see what I'm saying
How it doesn't make sense
How this entire system is hypocritical, it makes me laugh

Youniverse

Pulling the plug on a comatose isn't considered murder
The death penalty isn't considered premeditated murder
Wearing a blue suit and shooting black teens
Isn't considered murder
Bombing countries for "freedom" isn't considered murder
But abortion is

— *Circumstances*

Ritu Kaur

We are living in a satire
When is the punchline?

Youniverse

Perhaps the real gift
Is being blind
Being deaf
So that injustice is
Neither seen nor heard

Ritu Kaur

The less material things you have
The more liberty you have

Youniverse

I wonder how long Mother Earth would take
To heal from human destruction

Ritu Kaur

To be born a woman is to be born a warrior

Youniverse

People treat you differently when you speak the truth

— *Speak It Anyway*

Going inside anyone's house regardless of their gender
Black SUV's
Marble staircases
Stale duros with tapatio
Vodka
The dark
Asking to use the restroom
Not knowing where the restroom is
Feeling like I'm being watched in the restroom
When men snap random photos of me
When men tell me not to take their jokes seriously
When men tell me I'm mysterious
Men

— *Triggers List*

Youniverse

If I choose to come forward about my abuse
That is my choice
If I choose to keep quiet about my abuse
That is also my choice
'Cause I have to choose the right path for myself
But for you to blame me for choosing to keep quiet
For you to tell me that the abuser can go out there
And do it again
Is not in my hands
Those are the actions of the abuser
Because he is an abuser, a rapist, a criminal
And if I choose to come forward
I am coming forward for myself
I am advocating for myself
I am trying to get justice from a broken system for myself
And I have nothing to do with the actions of the abuser

Ritu Kaur

So many of you claim to be supporters
So many of you claim to be friends
But when I talk about the abuse that happened to me
So many of you supporters and friends keep quiet
So many of you cut communication with me
Ignore me in public, see me as damaged goods
Or worse, you discredit me, think that I was lying
You continue to keep ties with the abuser
Not believing he could commit such a heinous act
Whether he's your friend or family member, it doesn't matter
If you're not supporting a survivor when they reach out
If you're not helping end the stigma behind sexual abuse
Assault
Rape
Violence
Then you are adding to the stigma
You are allowing the cycle of abuse to continue
You are the reason why survivors stay quiet
You are the reason why survivors don't come forward
You are the reason why victims don't make it
'Cause not everyone makes it, not everyone is a survivor
You have to think about the way you think
Why you think the way you do
Why do you think the way you do?
Do you believe survivors when they're telling you their truth?
'Cause you may not have committed the abuse
But you contributed to taking away someone's voice
And that makes you just as much of an oppressor
As the perpetrator of abuse

— *You Are Accountable*

What were your expectations of that night?
Why did you go inside his house?
Were you planning to have sex with him?
Have you had sex before?
What were you wearing?
Was he barricading the exit door with his body?
If he wasn't barricading the door, why didn't you just get out?
How high were you?
Was he sober?
Did you tell him to stop aggressively or were you passive?
How did he take your shirt off?
What were your intentions?
Why didn't you scream for help?
Why didn't you call the police?
Why didn't you come to the police station after you left?
Did he finish (ejaculate)?
Did you see his erect penis?
It was dark?
Then how did you know his penis was erect?
Oh you felt his erect penis when he tried to hug you?
Why did you hide in the closet?
What were you wearing?
Why did you use the term coercion?
Why did you wait five days before coming in?
Why are you reporting this now?
Do you want him to go to jail?
What were you wearing?
What do you think he'll say if we bring him in here?
Are you going to cooperate?

— When Will We Start Asking Survivors The Right Questions? / Victim Blaming Questions At The Police Station

There is no female officer on site today
We don't do restraining orders here
We're trying to figure out....
If he was aggressively trying to have sex with you
Or if this was attempted rape
If you haven't formerly had sex, you wouldn't
understand sexual cues
He was not holding you hostage
You were not being held hostage
You did not escape, you snuck out
This is the penal code for sexual assault
We need to know if you're going to cooperate
This isn't how this works
You're a grown woman
We're trying to understand how he possibly assaulted
you
We ARE taking you very seriously
It doesn't matter if his DNA is on your pants
There were no witnesses so we can't assume anything
At worse he'd get a misdemeanor if he's charged
I understand what it's like, I've been on your side
It's going to be tough to convict him of anything
You should've screamed
You should've called us and left your phone on the side
We could've heard everything and came to you
You don't need a restraining order if he isn't harassing
you
We can't do anything if his family members are stalking
your social media accounts unless they commit an actual
crime
Delete your social media accounts
You're being uncooperative

— *Victim Blaming Statements I Encountered At The Police Station*

Youniverse

I walk into the police department ready to report the sexual assault
I walk out wondering if the assault even happened

— *Rape Culture*

Ritu Kaur

Why am I called a victim but treated like the criminal?

Youniverse

Maybe it's because of my openness
Maybe it's because of my welcoming personality
Maybe it's because I'm naive
Maybe it's because I give everyone the benefit of the doubt
Maybe it's because I believe what people tell me
Maybe it's because I dress immodestly
Maybe it's because of what I drink
Maybe it's because of how innocently I think
Maybe it's because I blurred the lines everytime I said no
Maybe it's because of all this I gave the wrong message
Maybe it's because I deserved it

— *Why Did You Let This Happen To You?*

Ritu Kaur

Why did he stay sober when I was intoxicated
Why did he not take me home when I asked
Why did he become dismissive when I almost cried
Why did he stay quiet when I told him no
Why did he plead me when I asked him to stop
Why did he hold me tighter when I told him to let me go
Why did he exert more force when I told him to get off
Why did he stay silent when I told him I didn't want to do this
Why did he keep quiet when I asked him why he was doing this
Why did he
Why did he
Why did he
Why does he not have to feel any pain
Why does he not have to think about what he did
Why does he get to live his life as if nothing happened
Why does he get support for being a criminal
Why does he get to go to his job everyday like normal
Why does he get the easy way out
Why does he
Why does he
Why does he

Youniverse

She called me my first day of training
But ignored me during the three months that I was unemployed
During a time that I had open availability
She wants to close this case before July, on her time
She wants me to come in today or tomorrow
I told her I just got this job
I can't just leave, my family depends on me
She says she'll take the abuser's statement
And submit it to the DA
I want to scream at her but I bite my tongue
I ask her if she can hold off until I get my work schedule
She says I need to let her know by Thursday
It's Tuesday now, my first day of training
I have two days to get a schedule I'm not even sure of
All while I've been waiting months for her call
That she's now trying to rush
Is this justice
Is this how it really is
A broken system where cases get dismissed
Where the victim continues to feel hopeless
Where the law says sexual assault is a crime
Yet it's treated like it's not serious
Where the abuser gets to walk free
While the victim goes in circles
I remember feeling this way as a kid in foster care
Like I had no control
Like I had no one to care
Like I would never see my mother
Like I was put in the wrong hands
Why was I the one abused as a kid
Yet still tormented by the system
Why was I assaulted as an adult
But when I ask for help
Not even the system that claims to bring justice
Is there to listen

What am I supposed to do when people tell me to smile
To be happy
That it'll be okay, that I'm strong and confident
Yet when I gather enough strength just to get through the day
I'm questioned if I'm a true victim
What am I supposed to do when I act as if nothing happened
And continue living my life
People question if this act of violence really happened to me
What am I supposed to do when I'm angry and broken
And I show it to the world
The world tells me to get over it, that I'm dramatic
That I deserved it because I didn't prevent it
That I should think positive
But when I think positive I'm back at square one
Questioned if I'm still a true victim
Going back through this cycle of judgment
Of trying to prove what happened to me
Of not being allowed to FEEL MY FEELINGS
Of not being allowed to TALK ABOUT WHAT HAPPENED TO ME
WHAT AM I SUPPOSED TO DO WHEN REGARDLESS OF WHAT I DO
IT'S NEVER GOOD ENOUGH FOR ANYONE
WHAT AM I SUPPOSED TO DO

Youniverse

How others perceive your truth
Is not your responsibility

Ritu Kaur

How many times will men touch my body without my consent
How many times will my home be invaded to violate me
To the point of dissociation
From the men who treat my body like it's a party
And not a sacred place
My body has become a graveyard from the pain
From the abuse
From the wrong people trying to put their empty hands on me
It is a cemetery filled with the hurt I've buried within me
From the bare hands that try to take away my wholeness
My body has experienced severe trauma
From the men who think they're entitled to a touch
A grab, a rub, *harassment*
From the 'brothers' who don't know how to respect me
Who don't ask me if I'm comfortable
Who don't respect my 'no'
Who make me feel alone
The same men who claim to love me don't really love me
'Cause they're not listening when I say this isn't what I was expecting
The man who says he cares but he isn't there
The ghosts who drown out my cries for help
The monsters who only love what I can do for them
Only 'love' me for how I make them feel
The men who don't believe me when I tell them I was abused
The men who need proof of my assaults to ensure it's the truth
The men who didn't believe that I was a 'virgin' for 24 years
The men who don't believe I've only had one sexual partner
Not that my 'herstory' should matter
The men who think they know me better than I know myself
The men who told me secrets that I would keep with me
The men who turned my body into a cemetery

Youniverse

They don't even sit at the same table as you
What makes you think they'll stand up for you

— *Expectations*

Ritu Kaur

What's the point what's the point what's the point.
There is no point there is no point there is no point. In
anything. So why. Why am I here. Why am I here.
Why am I here. I don't know where I want to be. But
I know this much. That I don't want to be here. So
why am I here. Why do I have to be here. Why did
the creator, create me. What's the point. What's the
point. What's the goddamn point.

It just is. What's the point. It just is. It just is
It just is
It just is

Youniverse

When I am frustrated with my writing
When I can no longer read it
Write it
Revise it
When I am tired of it
Is when I need it most

— *Patience*

Ritu Kaur

I love who I'm becoming
I am healing
I am strong
I am powerful
I am conscious
I am light
I am infinite
I am the youniverse

— *Affirmations*

The angels speak to me in synchronicities
111, 222, 333
I feel the flow of the youniverse within me
I love it when the angels think of me
When they guide me along my path and applaud me
How they make me feel less lonely
'Cause I know that they're listening to my fears and dreams
How they make me laugh 'cause they're funny
The angels are my guides
Lighting the way for me through divinity
Telepathy with my siblings, they are my sib-links
The cosmos never fail to amaze me
How thoughtful must my guides be
Always trying to keep me smiling
When I entered this life
I chose to have the best spirits around me
The youniverse blessed me with divine beings
The angels have helped bring light to my journey

Ritu Kaur

I see two men hug and leave
I think they're brothers
The person next to me sees the same thing
And assumes they're lovers

— *Life Is An Observation*

Youniverse

I miss sleeping under the stars

— 2008 In Punjab

Ritu Kaur

The things we do when we're faced with regret

Youniverse

The most inevitable truth in life is death
All of us
We're all going to die
You and I
As the time flies
Regardless of how we choose to spend our lives
The time will arrive
Isn't that enough to make you want to live life?

Ritu Kaur

The youniverse would be darker without you

Youniverse

Stretch marks are physical proof
Of your growth

— *Embrace*

Ritu Kaur

Light work is still light work
Even if enlightenment happens to just one person
And that person is you

Youniverse

If you're intimated
Please get out of my way
But if you're intrigued
Please come my way

Ritu Kaur

The truth makes people uncomfortable
But I'd rather have the truth than pretend like it's invisible

Youniverse

"Bless your heart dear, we all have to go sometimes"

— An 85-Year-Old Man Regarding His Younger Sister's Death

Ritu Kaur

We come to earth as teachers
We come to earth as students
But every single one of us is on a different level of consciousness
We all learn different lessons for ascension
To remember who we are and our life purpose
But not everyone will awaken at the same time
People come back for many lifetimes
That's the beauty and struggle of life
We have all of eternity to make it right

Youniverse

Allow yourself to be fearless
Or be afraid and get it done anyway

— *Fear Is An Illusion*

Ritu Kaur

When I read a poem
And wish I had written it

— *Beautiful Writing*

Youniverse

Urns for ashes
Gravesites for the deceased
Is it the dead who need these things
Or us as human beings

Ritu Kaur

If humans are the most intelligent inhabitants on Earth
How come we're the ones at war

Youniverse

Stop giving power to your past

— *Lifeless*

Ritu Kaur

Do the memories of me
Still haunt you

Youniverse

I am grateful for the One
God
Youniverse
The higher power
The light

— *Source*

Ritu Kaur

What about the ties that break in siblinghood
The ones that we grow up with and love
The ones who can understand us better than our parents
How we keep secrets for each other no one else knows of
How we fight one second but quickly make up
How we understand each other's hearts from the start
How we've seen each other's intentions since day one
How fighting for each other can quickly turn to
Fighting each other as we get older
Is it not tragic that the bonds we think are the strongest
Can sometimes break so easily because we age?
But don't we always see each other as kids
The kids who don't lose innocence
Is it worth being right if I'm losing a day one friend
A day one sister, brother, a day one sibling

Youniverse

Sometimes I think of the things I've said
As well as the things left unsaid between my sister
and I
How a single glance at each other
Can make us smile
How a single glance at each other
Can make us cry

— *Forgiveness / Soul Sister First / Blood Sister After*

Ritu Kaur

Two years after being on Earth
You made your entry on this planet
We laughed, we cried
We learned to share more than just toy cars and Barbie dolls
You were sensitive from the start
What a courageous trait
You went through hell but you always did it with grace
A creative soul
Teaching us what it's like to defy norms
You are a ray of peaceful light
Authentic and warm
You showed me how to use my voice
Without having to raise it
You've taught me to be brave
How can I repay you for this
I might have been born two years before you
But I wouldn't be here without you, Mannu

Youniverse

She cooks artistically
Everything she touches, grows
Her fingers dance gracefully when she moves them
Healing, healing, so much healing in her palms
How they create eloquent art
How they hold so much pain, so much love
How gently they wipe away my tears
And take away the hurt
How they hold all the powers in the youniverse

— *My Mother's Hands*

Ritu Kaur

The birds have returned

Youniverse

What about all of the beautiful things we see in each other
And never say out loud

Ritu Kaur

In friendship there is love
In love there is friendship

Youniverse

Karma isn't about hurting you
Karma is simple cause and effect
A law of the youniverse
What you put out returns to you in full circle
Maybe not in this lifetime but surely in another
It's why we suffer
Without knowing the root cause of suffering
We blame it on karma instead of our own
wrongdoings

— *Cosmic Law: Karma Just Is*

Ritu Kaur

If this is a parallel universe
This parallel universe is called reality

Youniverse

I still haven't found the one but I've stopped searching
'Cause for once in my life I feel full
For the first time in my life I feel complete
Like I'm not missing anything
Yet the topic of marriage comes up more often now that
I'm in my mid to late twenties
But who said marriage had to happen before thirty
'Cause if I marry it'll be because I want to
If I decide to spend my life with someone else
It'll be because we're in love
Looking at each other like we're at home
Where he'll find love notes in his boxer drawer
This is just a small glimpse of my love
'Cause when I love it's unconditional
And if I marry it'll be because I choose to
An active yes from my part
'Cause marriage should never make anyone feel like
Their life has come to a halt
If I marry I want to feel liberated in every sense
With someone who chooses me again and again
Where I feel a sense of security, a sense of peace
Can we spend time in silence comfortably
Can we talk about things where we disagree respectfully
Are we going to water each other to continue blooming
Are we going to speak to each other in soft voices
Even when we're angry
Are we going to have intimacy
Emotionally
Mentally
Physically
Are you just a fun Friday night
Or will you be my Sunday morning?

Ritu Kaur

I want to be so close to you
That our souls merge into one
And we are no longer separate
From one another

— *For Him*

I want to be consumed with love
I want to feel passion
It doesn't sit well with me
If love is on the surface
If love is testing out the waters
That is not love
Love isn't meant to be rationed
Love isn't about *ifs* or *buts*
My love is boundless
My love is healing
My love is unconditional
I'm either all in or completely out
So if I am not in the depths of love
If I am not consumed with love
Then I don't want anything to do with it

— *There Is No In Between When It Comes To Love*

Ritu Kaur

"I always have time for you"

Youniverse

Imagine having that telepathy with another lover
Imagine the chemistry
The passion
The wild wild love between sheets unplanned each time
You're a goddess
So why are you settling for a coward
And not a god

Ritu Kaur

From here to wherever the first youniverse is

— *If He Asks How Much I Love Him / Soul Mate*

My body
Not only looks like art
My body
Feels like art as well

— Lesson #1: My Body Is Art

Ritu Kaur

You don't have to suffer to create art
But sometimes the suffering births the most beautiful pieces

Youniverse

If you choose to stay
I thank you
And if you choose to leave
I still thank you

Ritu Kaur

Even if you're standing alone, you're still standing

Youniverse

Your thoughts are magic
The very specks you are made of
Contain stardust
You are the whole youniverse
In one vessel
How can you not feel powerful

— *YOUniverse*

Ritu Kaur

I am not a role model for anyone
But myself

Youniverse

Worship the woman
She is God

Ritu Kaur

I'm not afraid of death, no
I'm afraid of departing before my soul mission is complete

Youniverse

We are all a part of Source which is the creator
We're all fragments of Source floating around the universe
Living through vessels
Visiting different planets
Living different lives in the multiverse
Creating soul contracts
Choosing a certain experience to live
During a certain time
In a specific place
For soul growth
For learning
For love
Indeed, it is true
That we cross paths with everyone
For a purpose beyond human understanding
So when I tell you that you are the youniverse
I am not saying this as a cliche
When I tell you that you are the youniverse
I am reminding you of who you are
When I tell you that you are the youniverse
I am asking you to introduce yourself to yourself
And when I tell you that you are the youniverse
I am asking you to acknowledge the universe
Radiating inside of you

Ritu Kaur

I promise to make the most of
This life
This planet
This vessel
This power

— *Promise Me You'll Do The Same*

Youniverse

I have no regrets
None
Besides the pain I've inflicted on my mother

Ritu Kaur

Non-attachment
Is one of the highest forms of
Intelligence

Youniverse

If we heal earth
We heal each other
If we heal each other
We heal earth

Ritu Kaur

"You are poetry all on your own"

— From Meredith

Softness, always
Kindness, even if it isn't returned
To do as I please
As long as I don't inflict pain on myself or another
Not to take the leaves off branches 'cause trees cry too
Not to litter on mother Earth 'cause this planet is our home
To always tell the truth, no matter how harsh it may sound
Lies have no feet, that's what Mummy Ji told me
Regardless of how long it may take, honesty prevails
We all have a story, we're all hurting
To thank the higher power with each breath I could
Pure intentions in every step
Endless forgiveness no matter how much I hurt
To always respond with unconditional love

— How Mummy Ji Raised Me

Ritu Kaur

Every cell in my body has a purpose
So who am I to think I'm too small
To make a difference

Youniverse

The youniverse doesn't read our words
The youniverse reads our vibration

Ritu Kaur

When I used to read books as a kid
I never thought I'd end up writing them

Youniverse

You never know where
The waves
This life
Or this youniverse
Will take you

Ritu Kaur

Feel it in existence
In the now

— *Manifest*

Youniverse

How do you write? How do you create?

— I Speak It

Ritu Kaur

The youniverse reminds me that the paintbrush
Is in my hand
The world is the canvas
What I want with my heart
I can surely have it
No amount of wishing or wanting will get me to it
The power is in my hands if I can bring myself to it
The magic of the youniverse is within me
I am a master creator
A divine being
That came to earth to fulfill a mission
Then transcend back to Source after this division
The powers of Source are within me
I am the youniverse
And the youniverse is within me

Youniverse

She asked me if I could talk to anyone from the
present
Or past
Who'd it be

I told her
Sri Guru Nanak Dev Ji

Ritu Kaur

When we merge with source
We merge with one another….
So we'll never be apart

— *Infinite / We Are One*

Youniverse

I am a once in a lifetime type of woman

Ritu Kaur

Am I still someone you want to see in your last moments

To have people listen to you. To have people listen to the concerns of your heart. The concerns of your essence and how you perceive the world based on your experiences. To have people listen. To be heard. Is a form of love. To be able to move a room full of people through words. A blessing. Regardless of if you're a dancer, photographer, musician, painter, poet, actor, heartist. Art is where I've seen the most genuine parts of people. Art has no rules. It's beautiful because it's unfiltered. It's powerful because it's authentic. It's captivating because it's real. So please create. Please trust your work. Please share your heART with the world 'cause we need more of it. We need more heartists. We need more of you. Thank you for supporting my art. For holding it in your hands. For allowing it to be in your home. For providing it with a safe space. Thank you. Thank you from the bottom of my heART. Until the next birth.

— The Universe Says We Will Meet Again

Ritu Kaur

The light prevails

Youniverse

Do you miss my touch?

Ritu Kaur

When the final curtain calls
Will you be able to say you lived to your full potential

Youniverse

From the stars we came
To the stars we shall return

Ritu Kaur

Where the waves meet the shore
That's where you'll find me

Youniverse

With love and light, always

— *Ritu<3*

Ritu Kaur is an author, lightworker, purpose coach and heartist from the bay area, California. She published her first collection of poetry, *Waves* on October 7, 2017, at the age of 24. Writing has been an essential part of Ritu's life, as she has been intrigued with language and art since her childhood. At the age of 11, Ritu submitted a family history project which consisted of biographies about her family members; one of her teacher's comments to Ritu was "you are a sophisticated writer."

Aside from writing, Ritu enjoys traveling and photography. Ritu states "different forms of art and expression remind me that this world is a stage and we write our own scripts. We hold the power to create something beautiful out of our life stories." This belief is what lead to the release of her first book, *Waves*. Two years later, on October 10, 2019 came the birth of *Youniverse*.

Youniverse is about your universe, you hold the ability to create your reality. *Youniverse* is a 26-year journey of consciousness through experiences with narcissistic abuse, sexual assault, PTSD, love, heartbreak, loss and spirituality.

To stay connected with Ritu's writing and latest updates, subscribe to her newsletter: www.rituniverse.com. She also has a YouTube channel where she shares videos about spirituality, her spiritual awakening and more.